ORDINARY
SECRETS

Notes for Your Spiritual Journey

First published by O Books, 2007
O Books is an imprint of John Hunt Publishing Ltd.,
The Bothy, Deershot Lodge, Park Lane, Ropley, Hants, SO24 0BE, UK
office1@o-books.net
www.o-books.net

Distribution in:

UK and Europe
Orca Book Services
orders@orcabookservices.co.uk
Tel: 01202 665432 Fax: 01202 666219 Int. code (44)

USA and Canada
NBN
custserv@nbnbooks.com
Tel: 1 800 462 6420 Fax: 1 800 338 4550

Australia and New Zealand
Brumby Books
sales@brumbybooks.com.au
Tel: 61 3 9761 5535 Fax: 61 3 9761 7095

Far East (offices in Singapore, Thailand, Hong Kong, Taiwan)
Pansing Distribution Pte Ltd
kemal@pansing.com
Tel: 65 6319 9939 Fax: 65 6462 5761

South Africa
Alternative Books
altbook@peterhyde.co.za
Tel: 021 447 5300 Fax: 021 447 1430

A CIP catalogue record for this book is available from the British Library.

Printed in the US by Maple Vail

ORDINARY SECRETS

Notes for Your Spiritual Journey

Robert Y. Southard

BOOKS

Winchester, UK
Washington, USA

CONTENTS

Endorsement for Ordinary Secrets: Notes for your Spiritual Journey by Robert Y. Southard

"Turned off by lofty teachers, levitating gurus, and approaches to spirituality that require years of training? Want to start today to live a more productive, relaxed, ecstatic life? If so, this is your book. In it Bob Southard shares his 'ordinary secrets' that will send you on your way to an extraordinary life."

John Perkins, *New York Times*, Best Selling author of *Shapeshifting, The World Is As You Dream It, Confessions of An Economic Hit Man* and many other books.

"Bob Southard demystifies spirituality, offering deceptively simple methods to expand consciousness and empower a more fulfilling life. For anyone yearning to discover, express, and celebrate who they really are - *Ordinary Secrets* is a formula for magic!"

Llyn Roberts, M.A., author of *The Good Remembering* and co-author of *Shamanic Reiki*.

AUTHOR'S ACKNOWLEDGEMENTS

Every person we meet provides an opportunity for learning, for growth, for advancement on our spiritual path. I have been fortunate to meet many teachers and friends on my path. I wish I could mention them all, but they are all in my heart.

Of especial importance and support in writing this book are my family – my wife, Michaelene, my sons Gabe and Matthew and daughter-in-law Sarah, and my sister, Mary Jane.

Thanks also go to my dear friends, John Perkins, who taught me about shamanism and first introduced me to the concept that we are all one, Llyn Roberts, who taught me about Shamanic Reiki and other intangibles and was an invaluable source to bounce ideas off of about this book, and Julie Griffin, who taught me about hypnotherapy, another and important way to communicate with our higher selves.

I am also grateful to Dream Change, an organization founded by John Perkins, which provided me the opportunity to meet, know and learn from shamans and healers from many parts of the world.

1

INTRODUCTION

Have you spent the last twenty years sequestered in a Tibetan monastery studying from morning to night with monks, or hidden away in a cave meditating high on a mountainside in a remote location, living on bread and water? Have you had a near-death experience?

I haven't either.

But that has not prevented me from having an extraordinary journey.

I have been privileged to work with and learn from indigenous wisdom keepers or shamans, from the United States, Ecuador, Peru, Brazil, Siberia, Canada and Ireland.

I've also been fortunate to experience first hand, the energy and power one can feel standing on the side of Cotopaxi in Ecuador, the second highest active volcano in the world. I've seen, touched and assimilated the beauty and energy of the trees, rivers, plants, animals, and stones deep in the Amazon, the high Andes and Ireland as well as the United States.

Exotic?

Perhaps. But is all of this necessary for *your* extraordinary journey?

Definitely not.

Walk out into your yard or a park, visit a river, a lake, or go to a nursery or florist's. See, feel and smell the beauty and energy of the trees, flowers, rocks and grass around you. Everything you need for your journey is there, around you and inside you.

Interestingly, I came to realize not too long after I'd started my spiritual journey, that it was a journey about life and my path as well. It was a journey of discovery. I discovered that in opening my mind to explore my spirituality, many other thoughts and ideas crept in; concepts that once I'd seen through their veil of mystery seemed so simple. I came to call this process of finding the simple in the seemingly complex, revelations of the obvious.

What I hope you get out of this book is more understanding about your own power and knowledge, to depend on yourselves more, especially your inner voice, and how to focus on your journey. Some will read this book, do the exercises and journeys, and that *something* they *knew* but didn't quite get or accept before, will have clicked in. Some will get something, maybe more than one idea, and know it. Some will think I didn't get anything out of this, but they will have, it just won't be on a conscious level. It will become apparent when they are ready for it.

Another reason that I felt it was important to write this book is that few people in most social circles, including the family, will talk about their spiritual journeys or spirituality in a deep, personal or meaningful way.

I have discovered others on their journey, usually by accident. I was talking to a friend that I'd known for many years, and at one point I made a reference to my journey. She looked around to make sure that no one was in earshot and admitted, hesitantly, that she too was seeking her spiritual path. That secret confession opened the door to many interesting and fruitful discussions, benefiting both of us on our journeys.

A number of other people I've talked to are in a relationship in which the spouse or significant other does not share the same view or have a desire to even explore their spirituality. In fact, in many instances, it isn't a safe topic for discussion. Also many, if not most people cannot speak of it with others that they spend much of their waking lives with – their colleagues at work.

People often don't mention it because they could be considered weird, looked at differently, pitied, avoided or simply don't like to talk about anything remotely spiritual, especially if it falls outside traditional religions.

Another problem, of course, is that you can't prove much of spirituality by traditional scientific methods, so anything a person says can be challenged and the person can be ridiculed. A near-death experience is a good example. It can totally change your life and how you view spirituality, but you can't absolutely prove you've had one, even though your experience is similar to many others. An acquaintance of mine had a near-death experience. Without at first knowing it, he became a healer. When he first realized what was happening, he didn't understand it and couldn't explain it in normal scientific terms. He quickly decided not to worry about it and just use his newly acquired ability.

The exercises, journeys and meditations in this book are ones that I have found to be helpful, and are designed to be done alone. (Note: I will use the term journey as a catchall which includes not only journeys, but meditations and exercises as well.) If they are practiced with a partner, that can be helpful too. Sharing experiences can provide additional insights and teachings. I was alone on my journey through the early years, and found much success this way. But to talk about journeys is academic. To understand and learn from them, you have to do them. The more you do them, the more you understand.

It is important to remember that while I can present information, you have a choice about what you learn, accept or assimilate for yourself, as in life. You will learn something from this book, even if it's that a particular method, idea or suggestion isn't right for you. I've discovered that many times when I didn't agree with a thought or idea, it stimulated other thoughts that were right for me or solidified what I had previously thought was right for me – be open to this as well. I sincerely believe that if you read this book and practice the journeys, you will progress on your spiritual path much faster than you normally would. I would also strongly suggest and advise that you make sure that any thoughts, ideas or exercises are consistent with your beliefs and resonate with you before using or integrating any of them within your mind, spirit and body, in what I call your spiritual tapestry. I'll discuss more about this concept later. There is also no need to suspend beliefs or practices you currently have. As you progress on your spiritual journey, past, current and future thoughts and concepts will become part of you.

Most of all, I would like to share with you some thoughts, observations, readings, comments and revelations that I've had over the past twenty-five years or so while on my spiritual path, on my journey to learn more about myself, to discover who I am, where I fit in, and what I should be doing. I'll use my journey as an example, but this is not about me. The value of this book is not to learn about me, I'm just a small, quite unimportant part of the process. This process is about you. This book is about the process of your learning and traveling on your path, not mine.

Admittedly, I don't consider myself a shaman or a guru or a monk. Truthfully, I felt intimidated, incapable of reaching spiritual harmony because I wasn't a revered spiritual person. Then, I realized, I'm better than that. I'm an ordinary person who has had and is still on an extraordinary journey. Who better to help you on your way?

I am you!

It has taken me a long time to reach a level of comfort, my base camp if you will, on my climb of the Mt. Everest of spirituality, but perhaps in sharing my trip, you will be able to reach your base camp in a much shorter time.

Join me on this journey of a lifetime.

2

MY APPROACH

My approach to my spiritual journey had no order, design or road map. In fact, I didn't know I was on a journey for several years. Later, I realized that I have always been on my journey as have and are, all of us. But, in the beginning, I felt a need to explore, to seek out more than my traditional religious upbringing had given me, or that I had been able to get out of it.

There is no secret here; I read a lot of books, listened to tapes, took home study courses, attended workshops, went on trips and mostly, opened my mind to learning, accepting and assimilating from whatever source I could. What was particularly hard for me when I started on my quest is that I've been a businessman all my life, with very inside-the-box thinking. Things were black and white and tangible. Spirits and guides, energy, auras, chakras, that is, the non-tangible world, were difficult to understand or accept. With time, journeying and meditation, these concepts have become what are real for me. I rely less on the black and white, the tangible, and much more on the intangible.

When I was young, I was taught that God could be found in church and we should live as Jesus did when we were outside church. I was never taught that God was part of the trees and plants, flowers, water, air, earth, and us. I was never taught that we are all one.

Thus, my definition of spirituality encompasses traditional religion, but much more as well. For me, spirituality is the essence of our being, both internal (our relationship with God and our higher selves) and external (our relationship with people, nature and everything around us). I feel strongly that in order to interact with others, with community, in the most effective and loving way, it's best to be comfortable with yourself and your spirituality.

In the process of defining and assimilating my spirituality, I've also learned a lot about what might be considered non-spiritual states of mind, but which, I believe, are all part of the spiritual continuum. Some of these include thoughts on making choices, letting go of ego and others, or on how to achieve goals. These and other ways of living on this planet, and looking at life, have become part of my life and spirituality.

I know something has become part of my spirituality, has allowed me to take one more step on my path, to climb to and then pass my base camp, when it becomes integrated into what I now call my spiritual tapestry. I no longer think of it in terms of "I believe." It's more like, "I know." It is now part of me, part of my spirituality and it affects the way I think and the way I approach any activity in life.

I came to think of the spiritual path I was on as a spiritual tapestry, comprised of a series of threads of different colors and sometimes different thicknesses. Each thread in the tapestry repre-sents a thought from one source, a bit of philosophy from another or a concept from yet another. The thickness is determined by the amount of information or its importance in guiding me on my path. This tapestry will continue to grow as I continue to explore, being open to learn and assimilating newly learned concepts into it. This of course, is a metaphorical representation of my spiritual beliefs, but can serve to help focus on what is meaningful to someone. Writing this book has in fact, allowed me to focus, crystallize and more completely understand my spiritual feelings. I hope it will help you too.

I'd like now for you to take a journey to connect you with the boundless energy of Pachamama – a Quechua word that means at once, Mother Earth, the universe and time. While an ideal journey may take place in a quiet room, or out in nature allowing you to focus just on the journey, the reality of our everyday lives may not allow that to happen. If you are in a city, with horns beeping or emergency vehicles rushing by with sirens blaring, that's okay. Don't get upset by the intrusion, just allow it to be, and focus on your journey. And, if your mind happens to wander off the journey, that's okay, too. Gently bring yourself back into focus and continue.

Now, relax, and take a few minutes to connect with Pachamama.

Journey to Connect Energy:

Either sitting or lying down, please close your eyes, empty your mind, and take a deep breath…

Breathe in cool, refreshing relaxation and exhale all tensions, all worries, all your problems.

Again, in the most comfortable way for you, breathe in cool refreshing relaxation, and breathe out all your worries, all of the past, all of the future.

And, one more time. Breathe in the present, the here, the now.

Feel, as you breathe in, the energy of Pachamama flowing through your body.

Feel the universal energy flowing through every fiber and cell in your body.

And breathe out all of your troubles, all of your problems.

And now, at your own pace take a few more natural breaths, and just feel the energy around you. Feel the relaxation filtering throughout your body. Feel the beauty, and love, and power of Pachamama.

Come back to the here and now.

This journey takes little time, yet relaxes you, can lower your blood pressure and, I believe, opens up your mind to further learning.

Wasn't that simple? Didn't it feel good? And, it didn't cost anything. Why don't we do this for ourselves, once, twice or three times a day, myself included? Why? We don't have time; we have too many things to do. Maybe, we feel we don't deserve to relax, to feel this good. If you get nothing more from this book, and I think you will, at least make this part of your daily practice – and DO IT. Even once a day or once a week is better than not at all. This does not eliminate all your problems, or pay your bills, but it puts you in a better frame of mind to deal with life's challenges, and it's good for you.

Journey to Intention:

Please sit or lie in a comfortable position.

Take several deep breaths as before and relax.

Now, take a moment and clear your mind.

There are many ways to do this, but one method I use is to visualize a blank white board or blackboard. Focus on it, and it will empty your mind.

Or, if your orientation is more auditory, know, feel and experience complete silence.

Allow your intention in reading this book to drift into the emptiness.

Accept the first thought that comes into your mind.

Be with it for a few moments.

Keep this thought in your mind as you continue to read this book and do the journeys.

Come back to the physical world.

My intention in writing this book was that I asked for guidance to help others find their spiritual paths, their spirituality and, especially, to learn to trust themselves. I'll discuss more about intentions in Chapter 6.

I became convinced at some point during my journey, that in order to find the answers to my problems, my path, my spirituality, I had to find *The Way.* I thought there was only one way, and I just hadn't found it.

I think that this belief occurs because formalized religions promote it. Many wisdom keepers and workshop speakers, books and tapes will tell you that if you follow their teachings, you will become enlightened. I have, in fact, had shamans speak to me about the way things are, as though they are the only ones who understand and know.

I truly believe that most of these teachers are sincere in their beliefs. I have come to know some of them intimately, and discovered that they are just as human as everyone else (another revelation of the obvious). They have strengths and weaknesses as well as ups and downs just like the rest of us. They have problems on the earthly plane with financial concerns just like we do. They have their own special gifts, but we shouldn't expect them to be perfect. However, because they often come from a different culture, or country, or have spent twenty years in a Tibetan monastery, we tend to put them on a pedestal and believe everything they say.

I must tell you that I have the deepest respect for their knowledge and experience. Some have endured hardships and studied many years to achieve their status. Often, a guru tries to create an air of mystique, of separation. A true guru or shaman doesn't need to. Their humility and recognition that they are just like the rest of us, actually sets them apart. And, in the end, they are still speaking from their experience and learning, which may or may not resonate with us on our paths. In fact, everyone is unique. We have different physical makeup, background and experiences.

The bottom line, as we would say in business, is to take what makes sense for you and let the rest go – trust yourself to know what's right for you (see also Chapter 8).

Early on in my journey, I felt that if I didn't reach enlightenment through a particular book, course, workshop or CD, then I had failed. I came to realize that everything you do happens for a reason, there is no coincidence in life. I learned something from every approach, every attempt at defining my path. I have come to understand and accept that I may not reach enlightenment in this current lifetime. I have come to realize that what is most important is recognizing and enjoying the journey. I'll get there when it's appropriate and have great and diverse experiences on the way.

Have you ever wondered why there are so many different ways to do almost everything, why there are so many ways to cure for example? Among many others are aromatherapy, reflexology, acupuncture, hypnotherapy, Reiki and, oh yes, Western medicine. Why do we have all these different ways of healing? It seems obvious that sometimes one works for one person, and another one works for someone else with similar diseases or similar problems.

Why do we have different religions? I think that whichever Supreme Being is believed in, whether that Supreme Being is called God or Vishnu or pick a name, it's the same Supreme Being. Why choose one religion over another? Partially due to upbringing, to be sure, but when we become an adult, we can make our own decisions and some people do change. We choose to recognize and celebrate and honor the Supreme Being in a way that resonates with us. Again, this seems obvious.

How many different ways are there to get in touch with our higher self, our collective unconscious, the universe? We can do it through shamanism, journeying, hypnosis, Freudian psychology, and many other methods. Different people use different ways. Why? Because that way resonates with that person. It just seems right, and often you don't understand why.

It is probable that as we progress on our paths, we will add a particular thought or technique that makes sense at that point, and perhaps release another that is no longer useful or resonates with us. This is perfectly all right. This is your higher self or inner being making adjustments as you progress.

It is likely that a particular kind of therapy, thought process, or perhaps a series of questions, will help you resolve a problem. After it is resolved, you file that therapy away in your mental filing cabinet until another similar situation arises. You will have already discovered and used the tools to do so.

For me, after looking at a number of *ways*, I realized I was taking something away from each one, some a little, some a lot.

Then it occurred to me that this is *my way*. I finally realized that there wasn't necessarily just one path to follow, but potentially threads from many different *ways* building my path. *Your way* may be similar or completely different. You could find one religion or guru that satisfied your spiritual needs, or you could do as I have, and incorporate different beliefs to cultivate and develop y*our way*.

A simple example might help to clarify what I'm talking about. Let's use writing and the creative process. Some say that you should draw circles and follow one related item to another to develop ideas and story lines. Others would say that you should write each day, no matter what you write, just to get something on paper. Or, you should be disciplined and write at the same time and in the same place – your special writing place. You could walk or go to different places for inspiration; use sweetgrass or incense or some form of aromatherapy to help you write and be creative; or visualize a famous writer that you admire and imagine his talent seeping into your body. Some people use a pen to write with, others, a #2 pencil and still others, a computer. I could go on, but I think the point is clear.

Writers use different means to be creative, to get ideas and to solve problems in their work. Every one of the techniques I mentioned are valid for someone and I respect whichever way a writer chooses. For me, I use a combination of handwriting, then transfer to a computer, then make changes on a printed draft. I walk to help answer questions about plot, direction, or any other problem I might be trying to resolve; I write in different places, and write only when it feels right. That works for me, it's *my way*. Use what works for you.

We will talk of living in the present, being open to learn, setting intentions and so forth. Don't feel like you have to totally master one aspect we discuss before considering and working on others. Again, don't feel as though you need to suspend previous beliefs or change whatever practices you are doing now. You don't. Some old beliefs may change and some new beliefs may become integrated in your spiritual tapestry.

I believe that after having read this book, you will have the tools and direction to determine your path. My goal is not to learn everything about my path and purpose, but to confirm to myself that I'm doing what I should be doing and making the right decisions.

Life, on this planet isn't perfect and neither are you. That you try to live in the present, to let go of ego, that is what is important. When you find yourself straying from what you are trying to do at the moment, gently bring yourself back and continue.

If you wait for the perfect moment to do this or that, you won't do it. If I waited until I had more time to write this book, it wouldn't have been written – ever. While you can work to change your present circumstances, know and accept them for what they are and press on toward your goal – the perfect time is now.

Don't expect to be at the end of your journey by reading this book and doing the journeys. It is a continuing journey; the secret, and the fun, is to keep working at it.

3

THE PRESENT:

BE THERE AND BE AWARE

How much time do we spend planning what we're going to do with all the money we'll win in the lottery? Have you been out walking with your son or daughter on a woodland trail thinking about that rent or mortgage payment you have to make?

Is thinking about untold wealth fun? Of course, and many of us have very real and difficult financial situations that we deal with every day. Often we're so absorbed in worrying about meeting our financial obligations, that on our walk on the trail we miss seeing beautiful flowers, or trees, or perhaps a squirrel scurrying out of our way. Or, maybe we've missed a very important question posed to us by our child.

Why?

Because we're worried, we're thinking about something else. We've lost focus on what is, while we are worried/thinking about what might or should be. Try this simple journey:

Journey to Your Breath:

You can sit, lie down or stand – just be comfortable.
Close your eyes and focus on your breath.

Breathe in slowly and exhale slowly.

Again, in… and out…

Pay attention to each particle of air coming in through your nostrils, going into and expanding your lungs and then back out again.

Breathe several more times at your own pace.

What did you notice?

Probably that you forgot to worry about your bills. You aren't thinking about the disagreement you had with your significant other last night. In fact, none of your problems from the past or anticipated in the future affect you in this moment. You are focused on your breath and nothing else. You are in the present moment.

Notice how relaxed you feel. This journey can be taken at almost any time. If things are tense at work, take a couple of moments and do this journey. You'll be surprised at how relaxed you can get in a very short time. It doesn't make your problems go away, but it can put you in a better frame of mind to deal with them. And, while you're focused on your breath, or especially when you're out for a walk, you can't do anything about them anyway. Resolve to pay your bills or whatever situation is bothering you when you get home, and enjoy your child and nature in the moment.

When the present moment is over, it's over, you don't get it back.

I keep coming back to the present and living in the present. I've encountered it in so many different books and tapes. It is referred to as mindfulness – as the now, as being aware or awake – and has been written about in texts for thousands of years.

Yet most of us, when we are growing up, are never allowed to understand the value of the present because our parents didn't, and so the lack of focus of living in the present is perpetuated.

What does it mean to live in the present, in the moment, in the now?

Simply, it means to focus on what you're doing right now. At this moment, you are reading this book, so focus on it, enjoy it, get as much as you can out of it.

We can't do something now in the past, as it's gone by already, and we can't do something in the future, as it hasn't happened yet. We can do something in the present that will help in the future and help where we are, but we have to do it now.

It takes training, a reorientation if you will, of the way we've lived most of our lives. Keep repeating the journey you did earlier in the chapter until being in the present is natural for you.

Why is being in the present important to spirituality? What does being in the present have to do with spirituality? The way we try to access our higher self, our sub-conscious, find our path, or reach enlightenment is through meditation, visualization, hypnosis, journeying and others. We can't meditate in the past. We can plan to do it in the future, but we can only actually do it now, in the present.

Like many people, I get frustrated at work from time to time. One of the main reasons is that often I have so many things to do, and many of them are *priorities*. I know I can't do everything at once, so I start projecting or anticipating all the negative possibilities when one or more of these tasks isn't completed. The result is that little or nothing gets done (no need to mention this to my boss).

Usually, I'll remind myself to stop my journey into mayhem and get back to the present, to be in the now. Then, in the present moment, I prioritize and determine what needs to be done and in what order. It's like a small miracle. Because I am now focused on doing something in the present, I stop fantasizing about all the negative things that might happen, and actually plan and then do the tasks so that the future will bring positive results.

Another personal example is that when I am able to extract myself from the tedium of commute driving and observe the trees, plants, birds, even the unfortunate accumulation of trash by the roadside, that is, bring myself into the present, it makes the drive so much more interesting. I feel alive rather than tired and zombie-like.

We cannot, nor should we, ignore the past or the future. We can learn from the past, examine it in the present and determine what lessons we were given. Could we have handled a situation or relationship differently to result in a happier ending? Is it possible to take action in the present to alter that previous outcome? Whether there is or not, what did we learn?

Sometimes, although we can't change the events of the past, we can change our perception or reaction to the events. An example that happens to many of us on a daily basis is an aggressive or thoughtless driver that cuts in front of us when there's not enough space, so we have to jam on our brakes. We might carry that anger with us for miles, or hours. But, we can't change what just happened. We can, however, change our reaction to it. We can take a deep breath, acknowledge our feelings, and then just let it go. We've just taken a negative past situation and changed it into a positive present moment.

We can plan for the future, in the present, but the only time we can take steps to mold the future in the image that we would like it to be, is in the present. If you always live in the future, by the time the future comes, it's past – past time to do anything in the present to affect it. While you spend so much time thinking about how the future's going to be, you've missed the opportunity in the present to take steps to make the future unfold the way you'd like.

After thinking about it for a long time and reflecting on how I had gotten to the point I was at, I realized that not only was being in the present integral to the process, there could be no process without acknowledging the value of the present and that everything I had learned and discovered, I had done so in the present.

There is, however, a practical side to living in the present. I know of a young man who received five traffic tickets, five days in a row for listening to excessively loud music. He received these tickets at approximately the same time, the same place, and from the same police officer. One could argue that he was in the present and enjoying himself, just like I've been talking about. However, it's clear that he didn't learn from the past or plan for the future and was penalized as a result. Or, you don't want to be walking along a path and enjoying the flowers, then walk off the edge of a cliff. The key is to be there and be aware.

Enjoy your life, enjoy the journey and make the most of it. If there are parts you don't like, figure out what needs to be changed, change them in the present and the future will unfold in a more positive way.

Here are some practical ways to remind yourself to live in the present.

Journey to the Present:

Please sit or lie in a comfortable position.
Take a few slow comfortable breaths, inhaling relaxation and

exhaling all tension.
Empty your mind of all thoughts and emotions.
Take a few more slow comfortable breaths.

Now, think about the value of being in the present.
Think about how all actions take place in the present.

Think about what you can learn from the past – in the present.

Know that you can affect your future by planning in the present.

Continuing to breathe slowly and deeply,
Pick a thing, such as the sky, or an action, or checking your
watch, and let that remind you as a trigger to be in the present.
Or, pick something else that is meaningful and useful to you.
Resolve to change the trigger periodically.
Let these thoughts drift lazily around in your mind for a few
moments and become part of your day-to-day existence.

When you come back to the here and now, come back with a
resolve to live more of your life in the present and know that this
will help you accomplish your goals.

- Set your intention to be in the present in the morning, when
  you wake up. As with any goal you set out to accomplish, you
  have to want to do it to ensure success, anything less will
  likely lead to disappointment.
- Select a piece of jewelry, a necklace, perhaps, and every time
  you look at it, or feel it move, it acts as a trigger for you to be
  in the present. If you wear a watch, let every time you look at

it remind you to not only determine the time, but to be in the present. Or, perhaps you carry a stone in your pocket or purse. Each time you touch it can remind you of the value of being in the present.

- Making Choices: Realize that everything is a choice and making a choice in the present determines your future. Clear the path for the future, in the present. We'll talk more about making choices in Chapter 5.

- Other triggers could be: when you exhale or inhale, wake up, eat meals or see a tree. Even when your mind is clogged with other things, use that as a reminder.

- Periodically ask yourself, what am I thinking about? Am I thinking about something that is useful now or later? Am I in the present? If you're like me, you'll be surprised at how much time you spend thinking about non-productive matters. And, consider keeping a log-write down your thoughts at that moment

- When you hear a bell, ringing bells, doorbells, church bells, ice cream truck bells (if that doesn't bring you into the present, nothing will), bring your focus into the present.

- Set your watch to go off every half hour or other interval, to check your thoughts. Remind yourself, if necessary, to come back to the present.

- Put up notes in various places – the refrigerator, a mirror in the bathroom, the dashboard of your car. Vary what the notes say. For example, 'Be Present,' 'The Present is Now,' 'Tomorrow will be Today when it Happens,' 'Be Aware or Be Square.' Make up your own messages, have fun with it. Just the act of creating your own messages brings you into the present.

- Take time to really touch, smell, see and hear things we block out a lot, and thus don't appreciate what's around us. When you walk by a tree, really notice the tree, or touch it.

The reason for offering different suggestions is that some will resonate with you and some won't.

I'm not suggesting that you spend one hundred per cent of your time in the present. There will be times when remembering the past is good, comforting, or an opportunity to learn from what has happened. And, you'll need at times to think about your future and plan – in the present – about how to get there.

You may relapse, or you may struggle. Don't expect it to be easy; don't expect overnight success, that's setting yourself up for failure. Knowing that it won't be easy can take the pressure off. Be gentle, yet firm with yourself, but keep the goal in mind and visualize yourself as if you had already achieved it. Don't say to yourself that someday you'll be a writer, or, if you keep trying, you'll be a writer. Tell yourself instead that you are a writer, or in this case that you are in the present.

As I said in the **Journey to the Present**, you should periodically change your triggers. You may find that your reminder isn't working anymore; if it's become too familiar or accepted, then change it. If you're a person who lives by lists, then schedule your reminders, and schedule changes. Just that very act itself is a reminder of your goal.

Before closing this chapter, I'd like to introduce a concept that, while none of its parts are new, looking at it in the way I'm going to present it might be different than the way you've thought of the parts before. This simple idea will help you spend more time in the present, and can help you in almost any aspect of life. I call it:

F P I
Focus —- Practice —- Integrate

It applies to living in the present as well as meditating, journeying or working on goals.

- Focus on what you're trying to accomplish. Give it your full attention.
- Practice it, many times a day/week/month.
- Soon it will be integrated into your way of life. This applies to spiritual matters, positive attitudes, achieving all kinds of goals and improving your proficiency in sports.

The way this concept came to me also showed me that there was no such thing as coincidence. I was coaching baseball for my oldest son. The group of boys was in the ten to eleven year age range, old enough, I thought, to be able to pay attention and learn what I was trying to teach them about hitting and fielding. It got to be somewhat frustrating for me after a while, because I had to repeat the same instructions over and over. I couldn't understand why they didn't do as I'd instructed after telling them a couple of times.

Fast forward two months. I was attending a workshop in Florida and had a free afternoon. I decided to take a tennis lesson as I'd played tennis for many years without lessons (those who have played with me are painfully aware of this).

The tennis pro made a suggestion that improved my ground strokes immensely. I'd follow his instructions and hit a couple of really good shots, then forget and hit a poor shot. This sequence was repeated several times before it dawned on me – FOCUS,

FOCUS, FOCUS. Then PRACTICE, PRACTICE, PRACTICE. If I did this enough, the proper ground stroke would be integrated into my inventory of tennis strokes.

The professional athletes know this, of course, and that's why, whether it's tennis or baseball or golf, they hit thousands of balls until that stroke becomes part of the game. Having this revelation of the obvious would allow me to improve my tennis game, and teach my son and his teammates much more effectively with patience, rather than frustration on my part.

And, this same idea – Focus, Practice, Integrate – applies to other areas than just sports. For example, if you want to spend more time in the present, focus on that goal, keep practicing it (using the ideas I mentioned earlier or determine your own) and soon it will be integrated in your way of life. We'll talk about FPI later in the book in other areas as well.

Be there and be aware!

4

OPEN TO LEARN

When you are open to learn, you look at life and all that you encounter without the old filters, the prejudices or the judgments you've grown up with. You are aware that there is always something new to learn and that learning can occur from virtually any source.

While you are reading/listening/participating in the journeys, suspend judgment, set your ego aside (the ego that says I know this stuff, I don't need to do this, or it doesn't apply to me). Set it all aside and be open. That way, you'll get the most out of any situation; you won't inadvertently filter out information that could potentially be very useful to you. However, and this is critical, you don't have to just accept it, no matter what the source. After you've listened, absorbed and thought about it, if it doesn't resonate with you, then set it aside; you have at least given yourself the opportunity to learn/accept something new. It may have more meaning to you later on, or it may not be something that is ever useful to you. I can't, nor do I want, to make you accept, believe or use anything – only you can determine what's right for you, what thoughts and ideas should become part of your spiritual tapestry.

Early on in my spiritual journey, I thought there was an end point to learning. I believed that once I'd reached a comfortable level of understanding of my spirituality, that is, my base camp, then I could relax because my search would be over. There would be no need to attend any more workshops, listen to tapes or read any books other than the action/ adventure types that I enjoyed.

I couldn't have been more wrong.

For a couple of weeks after I reached base camp, I did stop all activities related to learning, to growing, to further developing my spirituality. But, there was a vacuum – one, I realized, that could only be filled by continuing to learn. My journey, and the development of my spirituality, had just begun. There was, and is, so much I don't know. I knew then that my spiritual journey would never end, a monumental discovery for me, in and of itself.

It was different now, though. The learning from that point on was done from a base of comfort and desire, rather than one of need, a very large difference. I knew that aspects of my spirituality would change and new threads would be added to my spiritual tapestry. Whatever happened, I knew that I would be doing and learning what I came into this lifetime for. I was, and had always been, as I now realized, on my path.

Part of the excitement is the learning and the trying, especially now that I've reached the first plateau. I wish I'd known that it was even possible so I could have enjoyed the exploration from the beginning. I truly enjoy reading, talking to people, listening to tapes/CD's, going to workshops. I love to learn.

I'm at a point now that even if I don't reach enlightenment in this lifetime, that's okay. I haven't changed what I do, just how I look at it.

Before we discuss being open to learn further, let's take a few minutes and do the following journey.

Journey to be Open:

Take several breaths, focusing on the air coming in and the air leaving – think of nothing else.

Now, take a slow, comfortable breath, breathing in pure, cleansing white light.
Feel this pure white light spreading throughout your body, cleansing every organ, muscle, fiber and cell in your body.
As you exhale, let the white light travel through all your pores, continuing to cleanse and relax you as it leaves.
Again.
Breathe in refreshing, cleansing white light.
As you exhale, release all tensions, worries and problems.
With your next breath, feel the universal energy coursing throughout your body, cleansing, relaxing as it flows through you, from your head... through your shoulders, arms and fingers. Down through your chest... abdomen... hips... thighs... calves... feet... and toes.
Exhale limiting thoughts, preconceived ideas and prejudices.
Feel the roadblocks to learning break down.
And again.
Breathe in once more, slowly... deeply...
As you exhale, know that you are ready to receive and assimilate any
knowledge that is available and appropriate for you at this time.

This brief exercise can be done at any time during the day. It is useful for preparing yourself to be open to learn, to focus on being in the present, and for general relaxation as well. Using this exercise at times when you are not expecting to learn anything can be especially beneficial because learning can occur anywhere at anytime and under any circumstances.

Often, you're learning and don't realize it. Every book you read, tape you listen to, workshop you attend, trip you take, wisdom keeper or ordinary person you speak with, provides an opportunity to learn. Learning can and does occur, whether you are aware of it or not.

Sometimes you learn that an idea or concept resonates with you and it then becomes part of your spiritual tapestry. Other ideas don't feel right or flow with you, but that too is a learning. Importantly for me, I have reached a level of comfort with myself so that I'm not a slave to someone else's ideas, thoughts or methods. I can accept some or all of what someone else teaches, and integrate it into my own needs and ways of thinking. As I open up more, I find that I read more, not less, and try to keep learning as much as possible.

How can learning occur?

When we read a spiritually oriented, self-help or how-to book, we expect to learn. Be open when you read fiction as well. There might be one thought provoking sentence in a book that could change your life. For me, just the act of reading, for example, Zen Buddhist texts is relaxing. I find myself in an almost meditative state.

We go to movies to be entertained, but even in a comedy, one line can be slipped in that can make a difference. The same is true of billboards, or television and radio advertising and slogans, too. In looking for catchy, attention-getting phrases to sell, advertisers sometimes come up with incredible sayings. "Be all that you can be." How many times have we heard this, and typically dismissed it, because it was an invitation to join the United States Army? But the source of it aside, it is a powerful and encouraging statement about a wonderful way to live life. I'm sure you can think of others.

Try this journey:

Journey to Learning:

As before, take several slow deep breaths and relax.
Enjoy it.
Relax deeper with each breath.

Now, take a moment to clear your mind.
See your mind as a blackboard, or whiteboard, and erase all thoughts and concerns.
Think about a slogan you've heard or read, something you've seen on a billboard perhaps, even an old one. Think about this slogan for a few moments. What can you learn from it? Is there something to assimilate into your spiritual tapestry, or know that it doesn't resonate with you? Even if it doesn't resonate, it is still a learning.

Try it again. Clear your mind. Think of a slogan, advertising jingle or a line in a book you read that particularly appealed to you. Remember, we're talking about a concept or idea; if you don't recall every specific word, it's okay.
Pause for a few moments and let your thoughts swirl gently through your mind.

Come back to the here and now.
Do this exercise periodically to keep your mind fresh and open.

This exercise is important for several reasons:

- You will learn from it.
- It trains you to be open – like a mantra.
- It helps you to be in the present.
- It makes life more interesting – instead of letting life pass you by in a daze, you're open and aware.

I find that when I to do this exercise, especially before driving, I think that I'll be more aware of billboards, but what actually happens is that I pay attention to everything. The trees, bushes, grass and stones I normally drive by in an hypnotic daze, leap into my awareness. I feel their energy and appreciate the beauty of the wildflowers eking out an existence by the side of the road. I feel so much more alive and arrive at my destination refreshed, rather than tired.

Always be aware!!

In spite of all that we do, should do, or shouldn't have done, there are lessons to be learned in everything that happens to us. It is usually the hardest lessons that we learn most from. And, we feel much more of an accomplishment when we overcome a serious challenge than a simple one. We think we want problems or their solutions to be easy, with little challenge, but do we really learn from those situations?

Here's a simple example: if you make one million dollars a year, to buy a thirty thousand dollar car is simple, you don't even have to think about it. But if you make thirty or forty thousand a year, it's a serious challenge.

My toughest teacher in high school, my Latin teacher, was Miss Lee. I still remember her after all these years. One of her favorite expressions was *"Namo Domo,"* or, "Nobody Home." I was the recipient of that expression on more than one occasion, but I still use the Latin roots today that I learned then. And, in a college psychology course, I didn't do that well grade-wise even though I worked extremely hard, but I enjoyed it the most and learned the most from it of any undergraduate course. Don't shy away just because something is hard, you will often learn more from it.

It's important to understand that we are always learning. I can honestly say that with all that I've learned so far, I've just scratched the surface of knowledge and spirituality – would it really be any fun if you knew everything anyway? It is also especially important to keep in mind that you don't know what you don't know. This is why younger drivers have so many accidents; they often think the limit of their experience is the limit of knowledge available.

So don't get discouraged that you don't know everything. Why else would you be here? Things change, one shift leads to other shifts and makes life so much fun. It's just like writing fiction. I plan it all out, but it changes as it goes. The characters dictate change, or the location, or scenes. I sometimes have to go back and change what's already happened to make sense in the present – it's fun for me because the story line keeps changing.

As in the other chapters in this book, the tasks presented and the journeys are not difficult. In Chapter 2 we talked about a process I call FPI, or Focus, Practice, Integrate. This works here as well. If you focus on being open to learn, and practice the journeys, you will integrate this idea into your being (your spiritual tapestry), and it will help you on your path.

Following are a few thoughts on how to be open to learn:

• Do the journeys presented here.

- Carry a notebook and pen – it not only gives you the means to record a conversation, slogan or other thoughts, but it also serves as a reminder that you are available for outside input.
- Look at everything with fresh, questioning, child-like eyes and ears. Remember what it was like when you were a child. Look for something more in a movie than just entertainment.
- Push aside the critical factor that blocks you from being accepting, that prevents you from being open. That doesn't mean being naïve. If you're open, you don't immediately think that something will never work. You consider it; you may end up feeling that it isn't for you, that it doesn't mesh with your beliefs, or that it doesn't resonate with you. That's okay, because you have at least examined it, thought about it, looked at it, given it an equal chance to become part of you as opposed to just eliminating it. Sometimes you have to hear something several times, or in just the right way, or at the right time to really get it.
- So much of what we do day-to-day is habit. This is not necessarily bad, but it can inhibit learning and observing what's around us. Try getting out of bed on the other side from where you normally do. Wear a different combination of clothes than you usually do. If you take a walk, go in a different direction or location. Be aware of any thoughts or ideas these changes might spark.
- Re-read a thought-provoking book that you may not have agreed with. Revisit it, or other thoughts and ideas you rejected in the past, without the old filters this time.
- Resolve to be more open as you continue this life's journey.
- I've found that life is more fun when I'm open to learn, and I think you will, too.

5

WHAT STATE IS YOUR MIND IN?

In the last two chapters, I spoke of what I feel are two of the key elements in establishing a state of mind conducive to becoming aware of, understanding and expanding your spirituality, living life in the present and being open to learn. There are other elements that also aid in this process. During my long spiritual journey, I discovered, or perhaps uncovered, several of what I have come to think of as useful discoveries or revelations of the obvious. Obvious, because once I understood them, they were so simple I wondered why they'd never occurred to me before.

I have found that integrating these additional elements or revelations into my spiritual tapestry and my way of living, have greatly facilitated my spiritual journey and my interaction with other entities on this planet.

I would like to share a few of these key discoveries in my life. Some may resonate with you and become part of your spiritual tapestry or may stimulate other thoughts and ideas that will be useful to you. You will, I'm sure, along the way, learn many other things that will be important in guiding you and determining how you live your life.

I refer often to these revelations or attitudes or elements as states of mind. This is not meant to imply that they are passive thoughts that just sit somewhere in your brain or sub-conscious.

These states of mind become integrated into your spiritual tapestry and help govern how you think about yourself and others and how you interact with others. They ultimately result in action.

There is not necessarily an order of importance. They are all important to me and you will view each one differently. The following states of mind are presented in random order.

Let Go of Ego

Don't worry, I'm not going to go all Freud on you, even though my undergraduate degree is in psychology. The ego is important. It is part of us and helps define us in this lifetime. So far, so good. The problems come when the ego becomes too prominent, when it forces its focus on you, or it, when it becomes all about you.

The ego is insidious, it not only blocks you from seeing reality, but it interferes when you try to listen to others, to your friends. It hinders you from understanding or empathizing with their pain or problems. It can put up a barricade to being open to learn. And, among other things, it can push compassion aside in favor of self-gratification. Everything becomes about you.

Shamans, gurus and mystics for thousands of years, and more recently even scientists, have told us that we are all one. We can conceptualize this, even believe it, but it is difficult to experience, to live it, because of ego. Our ego sets us apart, and believes that if we truly live oneness, it will lose its power. The ego can help clear the path as we try to be open to learning, or set intentions or apply any of the other elements or tools in this book, or it can be selfish, controlling and dominating.

However, I believe we can and should have it both ways. We do need to have a sense of separateness, of who we are, of our own identity. The ego in moderation can provide that and at the same time allow us to feel the unity with all other entities. The ego in moderation can aid us immensely on our spiritual journeys, providing a stable base as we continue to explore possibilities to add to our spiritual tapestries.

Try this journey:

Journey to Ego:

Take several comfortable breaths, focusing only on each breath. By now, this should trigger your body to relax to a reasonable level.

Imagine you are standing on the shore of a lake.
The sun is shining and the temperature is just the way you like it.
You see the sun reflected in the smooth surface of the water right next to your reflected image.
You feel safe, comfortable, and know that everything is all right.
You want to experience who you are without your ego running interference and putting its layer of self-interest on all that you do.
Watching your reflection in the lake, gently step back and away from your ego for a few moments.
You can now see the sun reflected in the lake, next to your ego and you.
Do you feel any different?
If you haven't already, allow your body to fill with pure love, compassion and harmony.
Enjoy that feeling for a few moments.

Now, maintaining your feelings of love, compassion and harmony, step forward and integrate your ego back into your body.

How do you feel now?

Do you feel your ego in moderation?

Maintain that feeling.

Come back to the here and now.

You likely feel relaxed and have more compassion for others. Hold onto this feeling as you continue on your path, and repeat this exercise whenever you feel your emphasis in life is too much oriented towards yourself.

Forgiveness

Forgiveness can be especially challenging. If someone hurts you, physically or emotionally, there is often a feeling to strike back, to seek revenge. Revenge is a double-edged sword, though. There may be some satisfaction in striking back, but it doesn't change what happened, and it usually doesn't make the feelings of hurt and anger disappear.

These emotions are damaging, sometimes more than the event itself. They can affect how you think, feel and act towards yourself as well as others. They are powerful emotions that can cause depression and affect you physically. They can cause your blood pressure and your heart rate to increase, and cause continuing tension and stress in your body.

One way to look at forgiveness is to do it for you. By that, I mean to forgive the person who has hurt you. Let it go, release the emotion or however you choose to look at it. By doing this, you are allowing yourself to heal emotionally and physically and move on in life, unencumbered by this pain. You clear yourself out and make room for new pleasures and learnings in life.

This doesn't mean you have to like the person, or spend time with them. You don't. But you also don't have to let a painful experience dominate your life. Recognize the situation for what it is, then set it aside and be at peace with yourself. It is easier said than done, for sure, but at least it's a positive approach to dealing with an unpleasant situation and will ultimately free you to continue on your spiritual journey, with a new appreciation for yourself for handling it in the best way for you.

Journey to Forgiveness:

Take a few comfortable breaths.
Allow relaxation in each time you inhale.
Guide tension, stress and anger out of your body each time you exhale.

On your next few breaths, feel peace, love and harmony flow into and throughout your body.
Push any remaining stress, tension or anger out with each exhale.

Now as you inhale, feel the healing energy of forgiveness entering your body.
Let it circulate throughout your body.
Feel the peace it brings.
Remember it.
Again.

And, again.

Come back to the here and now.

Embrace Change

Change is all around us and inside us. It happens every day – in small ways and often in large ways. It could be as simple as finding a different way to drive to work due to construction, or as complex as finding a new job or moving.

Even if we think we've eliminated change by doing the same things every day in the same way, we still get older each day and that is change. Everything, in fact, that we do changes us. As we continue to explore our spirituality and read books and journey, we change. We've spoken about how our spiritual tapestry changes as we add new threads and perhaps phase out old ones.

For me, change is a given; we can't stop it. What we can do though, is alter how we approach change, how we view it. If we embrace change, rather than fear it, it will happen more smoothly. It's the difference between driving on a flat paved road versus a dirt road filled with potholes. We can make a choice to approach change with a positive attitude rather than a negative one.

For example, if you need to move, rather than focus and dwell on what you are leaving, focus on what's ahead. You'll have a new place to live, an opportunity to meet new people, and new territory to explore. I'm not saying that everything will be just wonderful, though that's certainly possible, but look for the positive aspects and you will find them. If you always look for the negative, you will find that, too.

Embracing change, rather than fighting it, will help you on your spiritual journey immensely. At this point, I would usually suggest that you try a certain journey. Let's change that. I'd like you to design your own **Journey to Embrace Change**. Just relax, clear your mind, and welcome change into your heart, mind and body. And, perhaps, look at any upcoming changes in a positive light.

How do you feel?

Eliminate or Reduce Judgment

This is perhaps the most difficult state of mind to alter. We have grown up judging people. We've listened to our parents, friends and neighbors gossip and laugh at or criticize others. It has become so ingrained, that many times we don't even realize we do it.

What is the point of it? We judge others because of what they wear, what they believe, their sexual orientation, their color, how tall, short, fat, thin they are, how big or small their house is. I could go on for a long time. Do you notice a theme? If someone is different than us in any way, we judge him or her. It seems to me that the ego is at work here. It's not that simple, but I don't believe that we need to spend a lot of time analyzing every aspect of it. Perhaps, putting someone else down makes our ego feel better, but it truly does nothing to advance our mind and our spirit in any meaningful way. It does nothing to further our spiritual development or add to our spiritual tapestry, or sense of community or feelings of compassion. It can, in fact, lead us to overlook the rest of the person and some of their unique, incredible qualities. And, we can waste a lot of time that could be used doing something productive.

Try this journey:

Journey to Let Go of Judgment:

Sit or lie in a comfortable position.
Take a few slow breaths, breathing in relaxation.

Recall the last time you judged someone.
It could have been a friend or a stranger.
It could have been what they wore or looked like or what they believed.

Now, imagine that person looking at you and judging you.
How do you feel?
You might want to say "Just because I'm _____ (fill in the blank) doesn't make me a bad person, it's not who I am."
Can you imagine that person saying the same thing to you?

Did it help you on your spiritual path to judge or be judged?

Take a few more breaths and clear your mind.

Now visualize or imagine a parade of people in front of you.
You see tall people, short people, fat people, thin people, people of all colors and religions and wearing all kinds of clothes.
As each one passes in front of you, you embrace their differences.
Each person is good in their own way, even though they may be different than you.
Notice how you feel while embracing the difference.
Remember it.

Take a few more breaths and enjoy the feelings of peace, love and harmony that acceptance brings you.

…

Come back to the here and now.

Embrace the difference, don't judge it.

Making Choices

The various states of mind I discussed earlier may be perceived of as separate, and certainly, not every person will incorporate each of these approaches to life in their spiritual tapestries. Each state will have varying degrees of emphasis based on an individual's preference and needs. However, all of these approaches have at least one element in common – they are all choices.

We make choices all the time and often don't realize it. Everything we do is a choice – what to wear, what to eat, where to go on the weekend and thousands of others. Do we live in the present more than in the past or our imagined future? Do we allow ourselves to be open to learn from any source? Do we allow our ego to run our lives rather than be an important part of it? Do we judge people; do we have compassion for others? These are choices. What is important here is to recognize and bring into awareness each choice we make, that is, to take responsibility for our choices.

I taught a class for a few years about making choices. It was a class meant to improve driving attitudes and practices. The point of the course was to understand that certain, not so good choices were made that resulted in the participants having to take the course. Once the student grasped that, then they could understand that they could make different choices. For example, whether you drive at fifty miles per hour or eighty is a choice. If you're convinced that you're driving that fast because you're late, a better choice is to leave earlier.

Another example is aggressive driving, which I referred to briefly in Chapter 3. If someone cuts you off on the highway, you have a number of choices. Your first reaction might be, "That makes me so mad." Actually, your reaction is to *get* mad, the event doesn't *make* you mad. In the quiet of your home, you can consider different responses. For example, you could forgive that person, you could just make a choice to let it go, or retaliate with hand signs that aren't in the driver's manual, cut that driver off or other equally aggressive actions.

Pick the one that is least stressful to you, hopefully a non-violent approach, and rehearse it several times in your mind. Then when it happens for real, and it probably will, you will have a conditioned response. My response in this situation is to acknowledge the rudeness and feel comfortable with myself that I don't drive that way. Besides, in this particular situation, the other driver probably won't care and if you allow it to make you mad, you'll raise your blood pressure, your heartbeat will increase and your breath will speed up, none of which are good for you, nor will any of that change what happened.

Here's an extreme example: A person in one of my classes had just purchased a meal at Taco Bell®. He pulled out onto the street and was almost immediately cut off. He chased after the driver, pulled up along side of him and started throwing tacos at him. How many ways is this ineffective – and dangerous?

This process of identifying and rehearsing different approaches to an event applies to many other situations in life. Try this journey:

Journey to Choices:

Sit or lie in a comfortable position.

Take several comfortable, slow breaths, focusing on each breath.

Visualize or imagine relaxation flowing through your entire body each time you inhale.

When you exhale, imagine all anger, tension and stress leaving your body.

Recall a stressful situation that you think might arise again,

Or, a situation that has yet to occur and is causing you stress now.

Think of several different possible responses.

Review each possible response.

Consider the results of each response from emotional, physical and any other relevant point of view.

Place yourself in the situation and rehearse the response you've selected.

Try this several times, and if it feels right, use it when the situation arises.

Clear your mind and relax.

Take several more comfortable breaths.

Return to the here and now.

Another important point to remember about making choices is that while I make choices for myself, I can't make choices for someone else. I can decide that I want to approach life in a positive way using the states of mind I wrote about earlier in this chapter. Someone else can choose a different approach to life.

We do make choices in what we believe. I can't say to you that this is exactly how life, death and between lives works. I could say to you, "This is my hand." You can see and feel it and know that it's real. But, is there a spirit inside your physical body? When you have learned what you need to learn in this lifetime, will you move on to another? Personally, in my life experiences, I truly believe this is the way it is. But also, I would just rather believe there is more, since it can't absolutely be proven either way.

Coming to this realization has made the acceptance of death much more palatable. I no longer fear death, because it is just another shapeshift. I have also become convinced that it is most important to enjoy this lifetime as much as possible, to enjoy the journey, so when it is time to move on, I'll do so without regrets.

Thus, one of the most important points and encouragements I make in this book is for you to make your own spiritual choices and build your spiritual tapestry your way, not my way or anyone else's. This goes along with what I feel is another good choice: take responsibility for yourself and what happens to you in your life.

My way, your way – our ways constantly change, we're always growing and seeking, whether we realize it or not. How you approach or accept these changes can drastically affect your happiness in life.

6

TOOLS TO GET WHERE YOU'RE GOING

Throughout our time on earth, philosophers, scholars, mystics and shamans have told us that we are one, that we are all connected. Many have dismissed this as new-age mumbo jumbo even though it's been said and experienced for thousands of years. However, scientists over much of the last century, including Albert Einstein, Neils Bohr and many others have shown that we are not the solid, separate beings we seem to be, and thought we were, but that we are all energy, that at the smallest level of existence, we are all one. This level has many names, among them universal energy, zero point field, the matrix and the Source.

These scientists, and particularly physicists, have performed numerous experiments regarding the interconnectedness of all matter. A detailed examination of the different kinds of experiments is beyond the scope of this book (see *The Field* by Lynn McTaggart for a good summary). The findings in the field of quantum physics lend scientific confirmation to the unseen connections, the intangibles that I'd like to discuss in this chapter.

The intangibles I'll cover in this chapter are journeys, intentions, achieving goals and affirmations. There are many other non-tangible energy/spirit things or stuff, if you prefer, that happen every day, even though our senses can't detect them in the way that they can identify a chair or an orange.

My purpose is not to convince you that these energy things, such as prayer, intentions, intuition, spirits, angels, manifesting, affirmations, reincarnation – there is a long list – exist or have any effect. I cannot absolutely, scientifically prove a lot of these terms and concepts. Whether the above matters become a part of your beliefs is entirely up to you. I have my beliefs, my spiritual tapestry, and you will have yours, too.

Why is the intangible so important? While it's true that we can't reach out and touch it as we would a table, it does reach out and touch us in many ways. It gives structure to our beliefs. It guides us in ways that at times we often aren't aware of. Has a picture ever popped into your head giving you an answer to a perplexing question? Have you ever had a feeling or knowing that you should or shouldn't do something without knowing why you felt that way? Have you ever been in a situation where you just "knew" that you should turn left or right? Have you ever had a little voice in the back of your head or over your shoulder whispering, "Yes, it's okay," or "No, don't do that?"

Or, have you thought of a friend that you haven't seen for a while and then they call, or you run into them on the street? Have you or someone you know been sick or in pain and been inexplicitly cured, possibly through prayer or some form of energy healing such as Reiki?

We've all had these and similar experiences, whether we choose to recognize them or not. We can't see or touch the way these mysterious answers come to us, yet they do nevertheless. Energy related matters are much more difficult to convey to the ordinary person. Most people, for example, can't see an aura or feel the energy surrounding them.

To get some feel of the energy around us, try this journey:

Journey to Energy:

Sit in a comfortable position.
Take several slow, comfortable breaths, focusing on each one.

Relax.

Now, hold your hands in front of you, palms facing each other. Slowly bring them together, not touching, about two inches apart and then back apart to six to eight inches. Repeat this several times, in a gentle, continuous motion.
Do you feel the energy?
Many people can, and it's not just the motion of air.
Wave one hand back and forth to feel moving air.
Can you feel the difference?
Try this four or five days in a row. See if your ability to feel this energy changes each day.

Feeling energy is much more delicate than touching a table, but is every bit as real.

Journeys

Journeying, whether in the form of a meditation, exercise, practice or shamanic journey is an incredible way to relax and to connect with your conscious self, your higher self, your guides; it also provides numerous physical benefits. We have experienced a number of different journeys so far in this book. A journey is a tool, a means to an objective. Sometimes the objective is as simple as feeling relaxed and peaceful, and sometimes it is directed towards a specific goal.

You are by now quite familiar with journeys. The ones presented in this book are, on the surface, somewhat short. But each one can take as long as you like, by extending the breathing and relaxation portions, or simply by enjoying the emptiness that can be achieved in a journey no matter what its other purpose might be. A typical shamanic journey can take fifteen to thirty minutes, or even longer. Often, a journey will have drumming or music of some sort, usually instrumental or chanting in the background. This isn't necessary, however. It is good to be able to journey without depending on background support; it greatly widens the areas and circumstances that you can do it in.

One of the first questions that came to me when I started journeying, and a question I've heard many others ask over the years is, "How do we know if it's really our higher selves, or the universe, or just us making something up that we want to hear when we journey?" One way to help understand when we might be trying to deceive ourselves is to understand what it feels like when the truth is told.

Try this journey:

Journey to Truth:

Sit or lie in a comfortable position.

Take several slow breaths.

Focus on each breath, and as you breathe in, feel relaxation flowing throughout your body.

As you exhale, allow all worries, concerns or problems to leave.

When you are fully relaxed, ask yourself a question about something around you.

For example, you might ask yourself if the color of your hand is green.

Answer it incorrectly out loud, "Yes, it is green."

Notice how you feel.

Pay attention to any physical, as well as mental or emotional sensations.

Try another question.

Ask yourself if you're eight feet tall.

Again, answer it incorrectly out loud, "Yes, I'm eight feet tall."

Again, check on yourself.

How do you feel?

Remember the feelings you have after both questions – are they the same or different?

Next, ask another question and answer it correctly.

For example, ask yourself what color shirt or blouse you're wearing, and give the correct answer.

What are your feelings now?

Are they the same as before or different?

If different, are the differences subtle or obvious?

Pay attention to all the little things.

Does your brain seem to churn or hurt when you lie to yourself and feel calm when you don't?

Does your heart speed up or your muscles tense when you lie, or do you sweat?

Regardless of your particular sensations, almost everyone notices a difference between lying and telling the truth.

These differences are what the lie-detector test is based on, except in this case, it is internal detection.

Try this journey several times – each time reviewing how you feel.

Answer some questions truthfully, and others not.

Try it with emotional issues, not just physical.

Tell yourself that you don't like someone that you care for deeply or vice versa.

Do those sensations feel different from what you experienced before?

There may be big differences between the truth and a lie, or small, gentle ones depending on the question.

Take a few moments to reflect on the differences between the feelings you have when you tell the truth and when you lie. Remember these feelings.

Come back to the here and now.

This journey will help you understand the sometimes subtle differences in your body's response to questions, and whether you are telling yourself the truth or not. It will also help you to recognize when you are deluding yourself – for instance, you might be trying to convince yourself that your higher self is telling you that you will win the lottery. This journey will help you make that distinction.

Ultimately, does it matter where exactly the intuition is coming from? I believe that this is where our oneness with the universe comes into play. The answer, I think, comes from us, our higher selves and the universe. When you ask a question, you will get an answer. It may not come right away, or in a form that is easily understandable, and it may not be the answer you expect or want, but an answer will come. Through the continued use of various journeys, I hope you will learn to trust yourself (see also Chapter 8).

Intentions

As I mentioned earlier, it is much harder, if not impossible, to prove the effectiveness or merit of intentions or other ethereal matters using standard empirical methods. Studies have been conducted showing that praying for someone is better than not praying. But does the power of thought actually change things? Does setting an intention actually make it happen?

Again, while I can't empirically prove it, I believe, at the very least, it helps. I also feel that setting an intention gives one a direction, a plan. You set the intention in the present to favorably affect the future. This could be for a short period, like an hour, or part of a life plan. Minimally, setting an intention allows you to go forth with a positive attitude.

Olympic athletes don't enter a competition thinking that they'll never win. They have set their intention to win long before the actual competition begins. Whether they think of it in precisely these terms or not, they've gone through FPI. They've focused on their goal (intention) and planned out what they need to do to win. Then, they practice, practice and more practice until the physical motions and winning attitude is integrated into their mind and body.

Intentions can help you in several ways:

- Set goals, short and long term; if you don't know where you're going, it's much harder to get there.
- Setting the intention brings you into the present to help you plan for and change the future.
- It is better, I strongly believe, to look at life in a positive way.

You can set intentions without journeying, but I think that getting into a relaxed state allows your thoughts to flow more smoothly and assists in the more creative aspects of your intention. One of the most important aspects of setting an intention is not only to determine what you want to accomplish and plan for it, but to see the goal as if it were already accomplished. See it, and feel it, as though you have already achieved it. Integrate that feeling into your spirit, your mind, and your body.

It is popular today to say that you can do anything you want to do or be anyone you want to be. I would suggest some caution here, in a positive way. For example, if you want to be President of the United States in two weeks, that is not likely to happen no matter how much you want it. Too much of the process to get there is out of your control. If you want to lose ten pounds in a month, however, with the right attitude and approach (see the next section on Achieving Goals), you can do that – it is in your control.

Try this journey:

Journey to Intentions:

Sit or lie in a comfortable position.
Take several slow breaths.
As you inhale, feel all the muscles of your body relax.
As you exhale, clear your mind of all stress and worries and watch them leave your body.

When you feel sufficiently relaxed, allow an intention to come into your mind.
How does it feel?
Is it a spiritual goal, adding to your spiritual tapestry, or financial, or a relationship goal, or a physical action goal, or

something else?

See yourself as though you've already accomplished it.

Enjoy the moment.

Look back and see the steps you took to get there.

Ask questions of your higher self or your guides:

How long will it take?

Have you missed any steps?

Which actions that you have to take are the most crucial?

Can you do this alone, or will you need help?

Ask other questions that occur to you.

Now, sit with it for a few moments.

When you feel comfortable with your intention, and the steps it takes to get there,

come back to the here and now.

Achieving Goals

One of the lessons I learned on my spiritual path, was how to set goals and particularly, to be realistic when doing so. As I mentioned in Chapter 1, in my opinion, everything we do, how we approach life, how we set goals, is part of us, and therefore, part of our spirituality. And, we learn from everything we do, whether we realize it or not. Achieving goals is a subset of intentions – it is the plan for fulfilling your intention. The approach for achieving most goals is the same, whether it is an artistic endeavor, winning in sports, of fulfilling a personal goal, or satisfying spiritual needs.

I'll use as an example, one of the most popular goals people have today: losing weight. Have you ever heard any claims made that if you take pill X, the pounds will fall off, or you can lose weight easily with pill Y, or if you use exercise machine Z, you'll have abs of steel and lose twenty pounds in only thirty days?

Sound familiar?

If you then read the fine print, it will say something to the effect that these are not typical results. The results are also qualified by another statement that these pills or machines should be used in combination with a proper diet and exercise.

If you believe that using any of these products will make weight loss easy, you have already set yourself up for failure. This is true of many other intentions or goals. Believe in yourself, believe in what you wish to achieve, but don't expect it to happen immediately, or necessarily easily. If it does happen right away, that's great. If it doesn't, you've alerted yourself that it could take some time and energy, but that the goal is worth it and it will happen – in your mind's eye, it already has.

Important action items to achieve any goal include:

- Commitment: You must be committed to making it happen. A half-hearted attempt or commitment will lead to disappoint.
- Plan: You should determine specifically what the end result is and the steps you will take to get there.
- Maintain: Understand that there will likely be times when you don't want to continue, that your old habits will try to insinuate themselves back into your life. Part of your plan should be to devise ways to prevent this from happening.
- Visualize: Frequently visualize yourself as already having achieved your goal.
- Affirmations: Use affirmations (to be discussed in detail in the next section) to reinforce your goal.
- Journal: Keep track of your progress in a journal. It is easy to forget exactly where you started and the progress you've

made. A journal serves as reinforcement as well.
- Review: Set time aside periodically to know where you are in the process and to make sure you are still on track.

Here's a plan specifically oriented towards losing weight:

- **Commitment:**

Journey to Goal Commitment:

Light a candle, burn incense, listen to soothing music, or whatever else creates a relaxing atmosphere for you.
Sit or lie in a comfortable position.
Take several slow deep breaths and relax.
Allow all tension and stress to flow from your body.

Empty your mind – erase the white board in your mind.
Now, ask yourself: do I really want to lose weight – am I fully committed to it?
Continue to relax.
Listen to your inner voice, your higher self, your guides, and your feelings.
Trust Yourself!
If the answer is yes, you'll know you are ready to make a plan to do so.
Take a few moments and visualize your body as though you have already reached your desired weight.
See yourself in different situations wearing the clothes you'd like to wear at your new weight.

Imagine your friends congratulating you on your great new look.
Sit with this for a few moments.

If the answer is no, then you are not ready to commit yourself to this goal at this time and should not do so.
Come back to the here and now.

Losing weight isn't easy, no matter what the advertising says. Starting with the right attitude, a strong, positive and want-to-do-it attitude, is essential. If you aren't truly committed to it, and understand that there will be many challenging moments in the process, you may lose weight at first, but will almost inevitably gain it back.

- **Plan:** The plan should include:

Changing the way you think about food and exercise. Over the course of your life, you have developed habits and likes/dislikes of particular foods and an attitude towards exercise. It is, in most cases, necessary to re-shape these thoughts and attitudes to ones where nutritious foods and appropriate exercise are reflected in your commitment to weight loss. A journey can help you do this, make up your own.
Examine when and why you eat: stress/comfort; normal eating time; get hungry; snacks; taste; or habit, watching television for example.

Know that all these will continue to occur.
To understand your cravings, and the schedule on which they occur, for just one week, carry a pad and pen with you. Record

whenever you eat, the time, the reason and what you eat. All three are important.

Is what you crave and eat considered nutritious or junk food? Do you get hungry every hour or every two hours? Does the time change from day to day? Is the reason different each time you get hungry or is there a pattern? I suspect in most cases you will find a pattern around the interval of eating and the time of day. Patterns can be altered, for example, by stressful situations, such as when your boss yells at you, you have a fight with your significant other, a project you're working on doesn't turn out the way you'd planned, or any of a number of reasons.

Once you understand the pattern and the reasons, you will be able to plan ahead and prepare for each different situation in which you eat. For example, if you eat a candy bar when you are stressed, substitute a food that is lower in calories, fat and sugar, or substitute a meditation or some exercise.

Eat Nutritious Foods. In general, eat foods that are more nutritious and better for you, less of the foods that are not good for you. This should be done for all meals and snacks. Again, you need to change the way you look at eating.

Exercise. Even a small amount is better than none. For example: when you go to the mall, take a trip around the mall once or twice as part of your shopping routine, or go there just to walk if the weather isn't suitable to walk outside. Start with a little and increase to, some say 30 minutes, 5 days a week or X minutes, Y times a week. I feel it's up to you to decide, although using national guidelines can be of help.

The ultimate test is whether you are losing weight or not. If not, re-examine each part above to see where you can make further change to achieve the goal you have set for yourself.

As with any plan to change your physical being, it is important to discuss this with your doctor and keep your doctor advised of the weight loss and any potential side effects if they occur, particularly when exercising. Strenuous exercise after years of little or no exercise can be more dangerous than any beneficial effects from any weight you would lose. Caution, moderation and consultation with your doctor are highly encouraged and recommended.

- **Visualize:** Frequently visualize yourself as already having achieved your goal – see yourself at your desired weight.
- **Affirmations:** For example: "I like fresh fruit and vegetables." "I enjoy exercise and like to exercise every day." Make up your own, have fun with them and tailor them to your own needs and desires.
- **Journal:** Keep track of your progress in a journal. Record your weight each day and note any other victories, such as when you have an apple for a snack instead of a cupcake.
- **Review:** You may want to review where you are on a weekly basis. This is also a good time to reaffirm your commitment and to again visualize yourself as though you've reached your goal already.

One additional thought here is that with weight loss, as with many other goals, support from friends can be powerful. Perhaps one or more will join you, or possibly joining one of the commercial programs available would provide you with additional incentive.

With this, as with other goals, as with all aspects of your spirituality, your spiritual tapestry and your path, do it your way and trust yourself to do what is best for you.

Affirmations

An affirmation is a statement, preferably positive, which focuses on whatever goal, thought, idea or concept you wish to integrate into your way of life. Affirmations reinforce intentions and goal achievement, and can help you in living in the present, being open to learn, letting go of ego, forgiving, embracing change, letting go of judgment, and making choices. It is an all around tool that can also help you in other aspects of learning and change on your path. For example, if part of your plan to lose weight is to eat more nutritious foods, an affirmation that you would repeat several times a day could be: "Fruits and vegetables are good for me, and I like to eat them."

Sounds simple doesn't it? Too simple, perhaps, but affirmations can be very powerful and lead to life changing behaviors. Besides, the simpler we can keep our tasks, the more likely we are to do them.

I think affirmations work for several reasons:

- Just creating an affirmation focuses you on what you are trying to achieve.
- It is a reminder of what your goal is and can help reinforce your determination during trying times.
- Advertising is basically an affirmation. You hear or see ads promoting the manufacturer's product over and over again. When you want to buy a product of that type, if you comparison shop, you will, consciously or subconsciously feel comfortable with the product you have seen/heard advertised repeatedly. It might even encourage you to buy something you don't really need. But used positively, it helps you accomplish your goal.

- I also believe that an affirmation, if repeated often enough, becomes boring to the critical factor or judgmental part of our brains, which blocks new thoughts. When the critical factor becomes bored, the affirmation can slip below it and into the subconscious, allowing it to have some effect. At a point, it could change your thinking about a particular subject and you could engage in new behavior oriented towards your goal. Hypnosis, and my own HypnoJourneys™ (a combination of hypnosis and shamanic journeys to allow a person to enter an altered state to effect many different kinds of change), serve the same purpose, to get past the critical factor and allow information to flow more freely and change to happen more easily.

We have examined why affirmations work, so let's take a look at how to create them to serve your specific purpose. There are books, newsletters, tapes and CDs that contain all kinds of affirmations. They can be very helpful, and often you can find ones that are oriented towards your goal. However, it is easy enough to write your own and create the whole process in a way to be most effective for you.

Writing affirmations doesn't need to be complicated. As I've mentioned several times in this book, keep it simple. Here are a few guidelines, but change them or add to them as it suits you and your goal.

- Generally, the shorter the better, that way they are easier to remember and repeat.
- They should be positive. Would you rather repeat to yourself: "My body is too fat and I need to lose weight," or "I'm losing

weight and I look great." This accomplishes two things: it makes a positive statement, and shows you reaching your goal.

- You can use a visual affirmation as well. Picture yourself as already having lost the weight.
- They should fit the plan. As I mentioned earlier, "Fruits and vegetables are good for me, and I like to eat them." Or, since exercise is likely a part of your weight loss program, try this one, "Exercise feels good and I like to exercise every day."I could go on, but you get the idea. Make the affirmation fit your goal, whatever it is. Just writing it focuses you on what you're trying to achieve.

Other points to keep in mind to make your use of affirmations more successful:

- Keep the affirmation in front of you. Put a different one on your calendar every day; post it on your refrigerator, or your dresser. Put a note on your desk at work or on your computer monitor.
- If you've identified certain triggers that could throw you off course, place a note where you are sure to see it at this difficult time.
- Ask a friend to check in with you from time to time to remind you of where you're going.
- Set an alarm to go off periodically to remind you of your goal. This too can be an affirmation.
- If you're trying to lose weight, when you go to a clothing store, start looking at clothes that will fit your new figure.
- Be creative and place notes where they make sense for you.

Most importantly, you must be committed to it happening. Use everything possible to encourage yourself.

You now have plenty of tools to use to re-orient your life and spirituality in a way that makes the most sense for you. They give you the opportunity to take responsibility for yourself and what happens to you in your life and to give your life the direction you are seeking. In the next chapter, we'll look at ways to find your spiritual path.

7

FINDING YOUR SPIRITUAL PATH

I originally thought that I was writing this book to share my experiences with others. While that's true, I realized that I was also writing it for me, to summarize and understand where I was in my life's process and path. By sharing some of what I've learned, and more importantly, the process by which I've learned it, I feel that it can help you on your path.

We think that if we discover our path, life will be easy. I don't believe that this is necessarily true. There is much to learn and there will likely always be challenges or lessons in life. I believe that living on earth gives us a unique opportunity and challenge. It feels good to think about and focus on our spirituality, but we must also exist in the physical world and deal with the practicalities of mortgages/rent, food and other physical requirements. There is a practical side to life that cannot be ignored. I think that part of all of our paths is to work on achieving the balance between the spiritual side and the physical side.

But, for me, the truth is that I don't want to know too much detail about what my path is. I don't want to know that I'm to learn three things in this life which are A, B and C. Think how boring life would be if you knew that tomorrow X would happen, that next week Y would happen, and six months from now, Z would occur. What would life be like if you always knew what was coming next?

I am extremely comfortable knowing that I will learn what I need to and that the way I will is by following my heart, by doing what resonates with me, by feeling good about what I'm doing and what I've done.

For example, part of your path, part of what you need to learn in this lifetime may be compassion for others. It probably wouldn't be as specific as giving a dollar to each person you saw who was down on his luck, though that could be part of it.

It would more likely be a feeling that you need to feel more compassion for others. Perhaps earlier in this life, or a previous one, you hadn't felt this compassion because you were too caught up with yourself, but you now realize that you are only one part of the equation in both your physical and spiritual lives. The compassion you feel could manifest itself in many ways, small or large. But, it fits into your path in a broad category of compassion for others, not as giving a dollar to a homeless person.

Though I have reached my base camp on the Mt. Everest of spirituality, my spiritual path is not like a yellow brick road – clearly defined – where I can see exactly where I'm going and every turn is clearly delineated. I have principles and states of mind that guide me in making decisions and these decisions determine the path I take, to go one way or another.

How then, do you recognize when you have reached your base camp, that you are weaving your own spiritual tapestry, that you are on your path? I don't believe there is one crystal clear sign that lets you know you've reached your base camp. And I don't think the awareness that you've arrived will be the same for everyone. But I do believe that you are always on your spiritual path. It took me many years to figure that out.

I knew that I had reached my base camp when I realized that the idea of simply believing in something wasn't enough. In my base camp I had gone beyond belief to integration into my very essence. For example, to say, even to myself, that I believe in a Supreme Being (using whatever name you choose), no longer seemed adequate. I felt and knew that the Supreme Being was part of me, part of my spirit, part of my spiritual tapestry.

As I reflected on other thoughts and concepts that I had become aware of over my lifetime, I realized that I had assimilated many of them in the same way. They were no longer beliefs that were separate from me; they were part of me. There were many threads woven together to form my spiritual tapestry. They are my path and the sum of my spirituality.

This may be the way you come to know that you've reached your base camp, or it could be something else. It is to some extent, a state of mind. I don't believe you can just say to yourself that you've reached your base camp (see Journey to Truth in Chapter 6), but after reading this book and doing the journeys, you will know when you reach it.

Trust yourself. You will look back and see all that you've learned and come to understand about yourself, and realize that you are very comfortable with that level of knowledge. You will also realize that there is a greater amount of knowledge to be gained and lessons to be learned, but you now look forward to the learning eagerly, and with confidence, not with dismay or fear.

As I reviewed my life, I realized that certain events and feelings were guiding me to where I am today. For example, church itself wasn't satisfying even as a child. I never had the feeling or understanding through my church that God was everywhere and part of everything. I felt there was more to life and my spirituality than I had learned in church. That led me to look elsewhere; it created a hunger.

Take a moment now to look at your life. Ask yourself these questions:

- Does my current spiritual belief system satisfy my spiritual side of life?
- Do I feel like there's more to life?
- Am I happy with my life as it is and where I'm going?

My guess is that there is a hunger within you, one that you can't identify, a vague feeling of unease. And, you feel like there's more to life, that your current religious or other beliefs leave you unsettled, or you feel you need to learn more or to accomplish something. These thoughts and feelings have led you to this point in your life, to this book. You may not be destined to be rich and famous, or to be the Dalai Lama, there may be more basic lessons to learn and more fundamental spiritual issues to be addressed in this life, and that's okay.

I've asked myself, more than once, why I can't just go home and read, watch television, have a beer like I think so many other guys do. The answer, quite simply, is that it's not part of my path. I *have to* work on scripts for my HypnoJourney™ CDs or write; it makes me feel alive. I've always felt that if I'm never published or successful in the outside world, that's okay, because I'm doing this for myself first.

It's almost a cliché to say that life's a journey, not a destination, but it's true. The real secret to enjoying life, I believe, is to enjoy the journey, reach base camp and look forward to each day with an almost childlike anticipation of the events to come in your life.

Try this brief journey:

Journey to Anticipation:

Sit or lie in a comfortable position.

Take a few slow comfortable breaths, breathing in cool, refreshing relaxation.

Continue to relax.

Drift back to your childhood, to an extremely happy event. It could be a birthday or anything. It's a time when you are happy.

How did you feel?

Did you jump around excitedly, laugh, hug someone?

When was the last time you felt that way, or allowed yourself to feel that way?

Enjoy this feeling again for a few moments.

Now, come back to the present.

You can have these moments again, they are part of enjoying life's journey. When was the last time you felt that way, or allowed yourself to feel that way?

Most of the rest of this chapter consists of short journeys. I could go into more detail about my path, but it's just that, my path. Your path is different. You are unique. Some of the lessons you came here to learn will be similar to mine and other peoples, but your combination of lessons is likely different than those of anyone else.

These journeys will ask you to look at your life, your desires and your accomplishments from different perspectives. The combination of exercises should give you a good idea of what direction you should be taking in this life and will perhaps add additional threads to your spiritual tapestry.

From the learnings I've had in weaving my spiritual tapestry and the exploration and discovery of my own path, I truly believe that whatever we do is part of our path. We do have choices, and sometimes we make choices that are not in consonance with the lessons that we are here for, but there is a learning there as well.

In this series of journeys, each one begins with breathing exercises and clearing your mind. You will be guided to your chosen place where you can feel relaxed, in the present, open to learn and safe. This beginning process is called **Journey to Your Chosen Place**. At the end of this journey, you will be relaxed, your mind will be clear and you will be in a safe place. This is a journey in itself and you can spend time here in the emptiness, meditating, or you can go on to the other journeys presented in this chapter or others that you might devise for yourself. It would be best to practice this journey several times on its own – FPI – until you can say to yourself "Go to your chosen place" and achieve that relaxed, safe feeling.

I have listed a series of questions below. Each question or series of questions represents a journey. I would suggest that you do only one at a time. You may receive an answer during the journey, or it may come later. You should also allow time to process any answers, thoughts or ideas that come to you after each journey.

I feel that one question per day will work best and allow for whatever comes up to more fully develop. After you have asked the question, relax as you are for at least ten minutes (longer if you have the time). Then, sit for a few more moments focused on your breath and come back to the here and now.

Don't be disappointed if your guides don't do a Powerpoint™ presentation giving you detailed directions to the rest of your life.

It could happen that way, but it is more likely to be a nudge, or a warm feeling and you just know what answer you've been given. For example, if you asked the question about what you'd been doing for the last ten or twenty years, and you felt comfortable and warm or possibly tingly about your current job, for instance, that would be a good indication that your past activities had guided you to where you should be today.

After you have asked the question in a journey, if the answer leads you in a particular direction, then ask what actions, in the present, you can take to help move you in that direction.

I would suggest that the first time you go through these journeys, you do each of them over several days, one a day. You will likely find that some resonate within you more than others and you can focus on those as you continue the journeys in the days and weeks to come. You might also consider taping them to facilitate your journey and make repetition of the journeys easier.

Journey to Your Chosen Place:

Please sit or lie in a comfortable position.
Take a few slow comfortable breaths, inhaling relaxation and exhaling all tension.

Empty your mind of all thoughts and emotions.
Take a few more slow comfortable breaths.

Now, visualize or imagine a place where you feel comfortable, safe and content.
It can be a place that you've been to or one that you imagine.
It can be in a forest, by water, in your front yard or indoors –

anywhere that is right for you.

This is your special place.

For the next few moments, just *be* here.

Remember it.

Go to it when you have questions, or just need to relax.

Though you have access anywhere to your higher self, guides and angels, they will be especially available to you here.

Take a few more slow, comfortable breaths.

Questions and situations to consider when you are in your chosen place – remember, each one is a separate journey:

- Review events from earlier in your life up to the present. Are there certain things that happened that didn't seem to have any special significance at the time, but just bothered you or didn't feel right or you thought you should get more from? How have those events focused your present day thoughts, or guided you to begin searching or led you to look at life in a certain way? Can you find occurrences in your life leading you to where you are today?
- Another way to do this is to look back over your life. Look at your accomplishments: what do you wish you'd done, what would you have done if you had more time?
- What do you do that you *have* to do. Have you ever thought, I'm not sure I really want to do this, but I *have* to?
- Without thinking about it, what is the one thing you like to do most?
- What is your passion, what do you dream about doing?
- Look ahead six months, one year, and five years, continuing

to do what you're doing now. Are you happy with what you see? What is the best case scenario, what is the worst case scenario?

- If you read a newspaper article about yourself five years from now, what would it say? Then determine what you would like it to say and write it yourself.
- Imagine that you have one year to live. What do you want to accomplish in this year?

Notice that none of the questions came out and directly asked what your path is. They all point to your path in different ways and by asking the questions and presenting situations using different approaches, I believe you are likely to arrive at a satisfactory answer. Again, don't be disappointed if you don't receive step-by-step instructions. Your responses will most likely be feelings that you are proceeding in the right direction or not. Trust yourself.

A few other ideas that might be useful in discovering and following your path are:

- Ask yourself each morning when you wake up, while you are still a little hazy, in that twilight zone between being asleep and being awake, "What can I do today to be all that I can be?" You might be surprised at the answer.
- Also, ask yourself periodically where you want to be, how close you are to getting there, and what you need to do to realize your goals. Don't ask these questions at pre-specified times, surprise yourself with the questions and you never know what answers you might receive.
- If you have a feeling that you'd be interested in, for example, some form of artistic endeavor, like painting, writing or

sculpting, but you think you don't have time, consider what might happen if you spent thirty minutes a day starting today on that project. Where would you be in five or ten or twenty years?

- Also, if you are afraid to spend time writing out of fear of not being published, or painting because you won't be the next Picasso, why not just do it for yourself? You'll enjoy it so much more without that added pressure anyway.

You can't change what you have or haven't done in the past, but in the present, you can plan for the future you'd like and start making it happen.

I believe that everything you've done so far in life leads you to where you are today, and that this is your path. You are reading this book because it is time on your path to do so. You are ready for the exercises and teachings and to weave what you learn into your own spiritual tapestry.

I also believe that you can stray from your path by exercising free will, and by not listening to those urgings from inside you and from the universe. Although, even when you move away from your path, for a short time or a long time, maybe it's to learn a lesson that you needed to learn. So maybe you are always on your path, no matter what?

In the end, just as no book or tape or guru can tell me what or how I should believe or what my path is, I can't and don't presume to be able to tell you what yours is. You have that knowledge already. It's in your heart, your mind and your spirit. The purpose of this book is to help you to access this knowledge, to provide the means, through journeys, exercises and meditations, to tap into this knowledge, to bypass the logical portion of the mind, the critical factor that blocks your access to this knowledge.

This is a process that will take time. As you meditate and journey, along with being open to learn, being present and using the tools I've suggested, you will add threads to your spiritual tapestry, gradually reaching a point of comfort and a clearer understanding of what your path is. There is always more to learn and you will keep adding to your tapestry. Although a major breakthrough could happen all at once, as the advertisements for the weight loss pills say, this result is not typical.

8

TRUST YOURSELF

I can sum up this chapter, as the title implies, in two words – Trust Yourself. You have, within yourself, the capability to decide what is right for you, no one else can do that as well as you can. As I have done, you can read books, listen to tapes and CDs, take home study courses, attend workshops, take trips, and/or apprentice with a shaman or other teacher. From each of these sources, thoughts, ideas and concepts will emerge that you will want to weave into your spiritual tapestry.

But allow yourself, not others, to determine what is right for you. You know, but you have to trust yourself. This sounds so simple, as does much of life, as does being in the present, being open to learn, letting go of ego and other ideas we've talked about. Simple is good, but not always easy to achieve. Like other seemingly simple concepts presented in this book, it sounds so easy to trust yourself.

In reality, the idea of it is easy, but it does take focus and practice. You need to remind yourself frequently to trust yourself until it becomes ingrained. But trusting yourself doesn't mean that you ignore the advice or knowledge of others, your doctor, for example. Part of trusting yourself is trusting others in certain situations and more importantly, knowing when to trust others, of knowing your limitations.

If a shaman tells me that I have to believe XYZ, I'll consider it and may or may not, depending on how it resonates with me. If my doctor says that the spot on my back is cancerous, even though I don't want to, I'll accept her statement based on her knowledge and my trust in her. Or, if I had a broken arm, I wouldn't trust myself to set it, I'd let my doctor do it. I'll also let the NASA scientists figure out the best way to get the shuttle into space.

There is an important distinction between the physical and the spiritual. If I have a physical problem, my intuition as to the seriousness or treatment of it may be correct, but I will *always* consult with my physician for her diagnosis. For the proper spiritual thought, concept or idea to weave into my spiritual tapestry, I will trust myself, and confirm that it is the right one through journeys.

You've gotten this far in the book and you're almost to the end. You may be thinking now that along with some of the other ideas presented, these journeys are too easy. What's the catch?

There are two catches. The first is that while the journeys are easy, and the results can be profound, you must do the journeys and do them more than once. There's no set number of times, but you will know. I've been doing these journeys for years. Sometimes I have a new insight; sometimes I just have a nice relaxing journey. I'm okay with either result.

The second catch follows from the first. Set your expectations, your intentions, for success, but don't expect total clarity of your spirituality or your path to come instantaneously. As I've said before, it could, but it likely will not happen right away. It is a life-long process with information, thoughts and concepts coming when you are ready to receive them and integrate them into your spiritual tapestries. Besides, if you understood the totality of your spirituality and your path when you were thirty, what would you have to look forward to for the next forty or fifty years?

A key element here is not to put pressure on yourself to make something happen. That is usually limiting and self-defeating. Allow whatever needs to happen in the moment to happen. If there is emptiness in a particular journey, embrace it, as it is what you need at that time.

* * *

There is an analogy you may have heard before, but even so, I think it is worth repeating here because it is so relevant to what we're talking about. It illustrates our lives as though we were an onion. When we are born and in our early months and years, our minds and spirits are pure. We are open to learn, we love unconditionally and we live in the present, eager for the next challenge. We are the center of the onion.

As we grow and interact with our parents, we are told no, we are told what we can and can't do, we are led to think and believe the way our parents think and believe. We add layers of petals around our pureness, like an onion, blocking our access to our own thoughts and beliefs. As we continue to grow, teachers, the church, the government and our peers further act to convince us that everyone knows better what's right for us than we do. We are discouraged from thinking for ourselves. More layers are added.

Through the addition of these layers, our own access to who we are, to our higher selves is further blocked. We often become our own worst enemies. Many of us are filled with self-doubts and are timid and shy and feel we can't accomplish what we'd like. More layers have been added.

Hopefully, we will reach a point when we feel the need to explore and find out who we really are. We might not think of it in terms of our being onions, but, due to our early training, we feel that we have to look outside ourselves to get the answers we're seeking. I think that initially this can be very helpful. Others who have been through this process of peeling back the layers can help us begin to do so ourselves. At some point though, we need to realize that we can only go so far in looking at ourselves from the outside, from someone else's perspective, and that the ultimate answers lie within. Guidance from others can still be helpful, but once we reach this point of discovery, we need to develop our spirituality our way, not somebody else's. And that is the point of this book, to explore your way, to add to your spiritual tapestry in your way, not mine or anyone else's. And most importantly, I encourage you to trust yourself.

Caution: as you explore your inner self, you will likely discover thoughts, concepts and beliefs that are different than the ones you grew up with, no matter what spiritual or religious background you are familiar with. You will be tempted at times, no, challenged, to alter those old beliefs. You will find that new thoughts may take you out of that comfortable belief system and take you into, what is for you, unknown and uncharted territory. Peeling back the petals of the onion surrounding you will be difficult at times. You might feel guilty, you might long for the comfort of the past when you didn't have to think, when you were told what was right for you and how to believe.

Trust yourself. It might be frightening at times, but if you trust yourself and look deep inside, you'll see that you are able to and you will make the right decision for what you need. It's much like the lottery; you have to play to win. In the area of the heart and your spirituality, you have so much more to win than just money.

To help get past and through your outer layers and uncover your spirituality and access to your higher self, we've covered a number of different journeys throughout this book. Now, as part of trusting yourself and developing *your way*, I'd like to talk about designing your own journeys, ones that fit your needs and your way of thinking and believing. You can tailor them to your particular needs at any point in time.

The basic format of a journey is simple:

• Relax. This can consist of:
Taking several slow comfortable deep breaths.
Focusing on your breath.
Visualizing or imagining a white light flowing through your body from your crown chakra at the top of your head, down and out through your toes, relaxing and healing as it travels down your body.
Feeling all tension, stress and anxiety leaving your body as you exhale.
You can go to your chosen place, or go to any other spot where you feel comfortable.
You may wish to use background music or drumming, or nothing depending on where you are, how you feel or what you are trying to accomplish.
You may also find it beneficial to change your relaxation script and background from time to time. For some, using the same language all the time can become routine and lose some of its relaxing effects. For others, the same language provides comfort and allows the relaxation to occur smoothly and quickly.

- Therapy or Message.

What are you trying to accomplish? What message do you want to get to your subconscious? What questions do you want to ask your higher self or the universe?

The message can set intentions about anything you want, whatever is concerning you or you are focused on at the time. Or, your message can be no message. Perhaps you just need to go into the emptiness. Perhaps you just want to experience peace or to clear your mind of worries or tension or stress, at least for a short time. That's wonderful, do it. It's your message, do what you want with it, and do what you need.

Your language here can be similar, or in some cases, identical to affirmations. It is important that any statements made are positive and that they reflect that you are successful at what you're trying to achieve.

If you ask a question, don't try to force an answer, just let it come. It may not happen in the time frame or way that you would like, but it will come.

- Return.

Come back to the present, to the here and now.

Give yourself some pleasant thoughts or positive affirmations or just come back to the present. There is no pressure to perform or do anything, this is your journey. Again, each part will likely differ each time you do it, depending on your needs at the time, and that's okay.

I recommend that you allow yourself a few minutes after taking any of the journeys before driving a car or operating any kind of machinery so that you can be fully in the present before undertaking these activities.

The journeys I've spoken of in this book are not the only kind, of course. Walking can be a great way to relax. You can clear your mind and just enjoy the scenery or the emptiness surrounding each leaf or branch or flower. I use walking to answer questions, particularly when I'm writing and have a block of some sort, or I'm trying to figure out what comes next. I always get an answer. Sitting somewhere, anywhere – just being, can be incredibly relaxing and refreshing. I have a picture on the wall facing my bed that has a path in the woods leading to a small cottage. Just looking at that is relaxing.

Find what works for you. Have a playbook of journeys to use for different purposes and different situations. You will know what is right for you each time and will become more comfortable with this process the more you do it.

Due to our training at an early age, we tend to look for a set of rules that will tell us how to live, how to contact God, or how to define our spirituality – the onion. The true answer to these questions is inside ourselves: our spirit, higher self, inner being, intuition, or whatever you choose to call it. For me, reading books, listening to tapes, taking workshops or home study courses, or going on trips triggers my inner being to pick out what I need at the time. Often, if you're talking to someone who's read the same book as you, that person might say, "I liked the part where…" You might reply, "I don't remember that part, but I thought…" Same book, same words, but you each needed and received something different.

To trust yourself is to know that you will get from each encounter – whether it be a book, tape, workshop, wisdom keeper or your inner being – what you need. It will not necessarily be what someone else gets using the same sources or their own inner being.

Listen to yourself. Here's a case in point. My father transitioned to the other side many years ago. I never felt compelled to go to the gravesite. I didn't know why at the time. Part of me had these unformed and unfocused thoughts about the difference between the physical body and the spiritual body, but at that time I couldn't bring those thoughts to resolution. I also felt badly about it, that there was something wrong with me, because so many other people did visit their deceased loved ones' gravesites.

Years later, when I realized that our spiritual beings came to use these physical bodies to learn whatever lessons we needed to, then transitioned back, it all made sense. The reason that I didn't then and still don't now feel it necessary to visit his grave is that my father, the spirit, lives on and certainly isn't at his gravesite in any event. You may feel differently, and that's perfectly okay.

In the end, know you are on your path – you may want to reassure yourself of that, but regardless of how much or how little you know about your path, you are on it.

When you allow yourself to be who you are and work in resonance with yourself, you will be aligned with your higher self, and your purpose here during this visit to earth. You will find that you will accomplish more with less effort if you are in resonance with your higher self – and get ego out of the way. Let love be your guide, let your higher self be your guide. You are on your path now and will learn what you need to.

Don't expect it to be easy. Don't expect it to happen overnight or immediately. It will take time. There will be ups and downs. I've known shamans well, shamans who have practiced their art for many years. As knowledgeable as they are, they are still subject to the problems and frailties of all human beings. Don't be harsh with yourself. Try to do your best and to learn and improve.

There are tools in this book to help you on your path, to help you find your way. Use them. Know that you will get to where you need to be. On days and at times your life doesn't go as you would like, you can journey to reassure yourself that you are where you should be, that this less than perfect day is likely providing you with a lesson.

I hope that if you get nothing else from this book, you will have learned to trust your judgment and to know that you are the best person to determine what your spirituality should be. Some look forward to the goal, but don't enjoy the process. We will spend a lifetime on the process; use the journeys to help you enjoy it.

Find your way, it is there inside you, waiting.

Trust Yourself!

BIBLIOGRAPHY

Baumann, T. Lee, M.D. *God at the Speed of Light.* Virginia Beach, VA: A.R.E. Press, 2001.

Bruce, Eve, M.D. *Shaman, M.D.* Rochester, Vermont: Destiny Books, 2002.

Easwaran, Eknath. *The Bhagavad Gita.* Petaluma, California: Nilgiri Press, 1985.

Easwaran, Eknath. *The Dhammapada.* Petaluma, California: Nilgiri Press, 1986.

Hahn, Thich Nhat. *The Miracle of Mindfulness.* Boston: Beacon Press, 1987.

Johnson, Spencer. *The Present.* New York: Doubleday, 2003.

Kaufman, Barry Neil. *Happiness Is A Choice.* New York: Fawcett Columbine, 1991.

Laszlo, Ervin. *Science and the Akashic Field: An Integral Theory of Everything.* Rochester, Vermont: Inner Traditions, 2004.

McTaggart, Lynne. *The Field.* New York: Harper Perennial, 2002.

Newton, Michael, Ph.D. *Journey of Souls.* St. Paul, Minnesota: Llewellyn Publications, 2002.

Perkins, John. *The World Is As You Dream It.* Rochester, Vermont: Destiny Books, 1994.

Perkins, John. *Shapeshifting.* Rochester, Vermont: Destiny Books, 1997.

Roberts, Llyn. *The Good Remembering.* Winchester, U.K., New York: O Books, 2007.

Roberts, Llyn and Levy, Robert. *Shamanic Reiki.* Winchester, U.K., New York: O Books, 2007.

ABOUT THE AUTHOR

Bob is a businessman with a B.S. in Psychology and an M.B.A. He is a Certified Hypnotherapist, Shamanic Reiki Master Practitioner, and has worked with a number of shamans in the United States, the highlands of Ecuador and the Amazon for many years. Bob currently sits on the Dream Change board of directors.

He also developed the HypnoJourney™, a combination of ancient and traditional shamanic journeying practices with more modern hypnosis techniques, after more than ten years of study and practice in shamanic journeying and hypnosis. He offers workshops featuring the HypnoJourney™ process and produces HypnoJourney™ CDs so people can benefit from this practice on their own.

He lives in eastern Massachusetts in the U.S. and writes fiction as well as non-fiction. For more information about Bob Southard and his work and to learn about Dream Change:

www.bostonmystery.com and www.dreamchange.org

O books
O is a symbol of the world, of oneness and unity. In different cultures it also means the "eye", symbolizing knowledge and insight, and in Old English it means "place of love or home". O books explores the many paths of understanding which different traditions have developed down the ages, particularly those today that express respect for the planet and all of life. In philosophy, metaphysics and aesthetics O as zero relates to infinity, indivisibility and fate. In Zero Books we are developing a list of provocative shorter titles that cross different specializations and challenge conventional academic or majority opinion.

For more information on the full list of over 300 titles please visit our website
www.O-books.net

myspiritradio is an exciting web, internet, podcast and mobile phone global broadcast network for all those interested in teaching and learning in the fields of body, mind, spirit and self development. Listeners can hear the show online via computer or mobile phone, and even download their favourite shows to listen to on MP3 players whilst driving, working, or relaxing.

Feed your mind, change your life with O Books,
The O Books radio programme carries interviews with most authors, sharing their wisdom on life, the universe and everything...e mail questions and co-create the show with O Books and myspiritradio.

Just visit **www.myspiritradio.com** for more information.

RECENT O BOOKS

Back to the Truth
5,000 years of Advaita

Dennis Waite

A wonderful book. Encyclopedic in nature, and destined to become a classic. **James Braha**

Absolutely brilliant...an ease of writing with a water-tight argument outlining the great universal truths. This book will become a modern classic. A milestone in the history of Advaita. **Paula Marvelly**

1905047614 500pp **£19.95 $29.95**

Beyond Photography
Encounters with orbs, angels and mysterious light forms

Katie Hall and John Pickering

The authors invite you to join them on a fascinating quest; a voyage of discovery into the nature of a phenomenon, manifestations of which are shown as being historical and global as well as contemporary and intently personal.

At journey's end you may find yourself a believer, a doubter or simply an intrigued wonderer... Whatever the outcome, the process of journeying is likely prove provocative and stimulating and - as with the mysterious images fleetingly captured by the authors' cameras - inspiring and potentially enlightening. **Brian Sibley**, author and broadcaster.

1905047908 272pp 50 b/w photos +8pp colour insert **£12.99 $24.95**

Don't Get MAD Get Wise
Why no one ever makes you angry, ever!

Mike George

There is a journey we all need to make, from anger, to peace, to forgiveness. Anger always destroys, peace always restores, and forgiveness always heals. This explains the journey, the steps you can take to make it happen for you.

1905047827 160pp **£7.99 $14.95**

IF You Fall...

It's a new beginning

Karen Darke

Karen Darke's story is about the indomitability of spirit, from one of life's cruel vagaries of fortune to what is insight and inspiration. She has overcome the limitations of paralysis and discovered a life of challenge and adventure that many of us only dream about. It is all about the mind, the spirit and the desire that some of us find, but which all of us possess.

Joe Simpson, mountaineer and author of *Touching the Void*

1905047886 240pp **£9.99 $19.95**

Love, Healing and Happiness

Spiritual wisdom for a post-secular era

Larry Culliford

This will become a classic book on spirituality. It is immensely practical and grounded. It mirrors the author's compassion and lays the foundation for a higher understanding of human suffering and hope. **Reinhard Kowalski** Consultant Clinical Psychologist

1905047916 304pp £10.99 $19.95

A Map to God

Awakening Spiritual Integrity

Susie Anthony

This describes an ancient hermetic pathway, representing a golden thread running through many traditions, which offers all we need to understand

and do to actually become our best selves.

1846940443 260pp **£10.99 $21.95**

Punk Science
Inside the mind of God
Manjir Samanta-Laughton

Wow! Punk Science is an extraordinary journey from the microcosm of the atom to the macrocosm of the Universe and all stops in between. Manjir Samanta-Laughton's synthesis of cosmology and consciousness is sheer genius. It is elegant, simple and, as an added bonus, makes great reading. **Dr Bruce H. Lipton**, author of *The Biology of Belief*

1905047932 320pp **£12.95 $22.95**

Rosslyn Revealed
A secret library in stone
Alan Butler

Rosslyn Revealed gets to the bottom of the mystery of the chapel featured in the Da Vinci Code. The results of a lifetime of careful research and study demonstrate that truth really is stranger than fiction; a library of philosophical ideas and mystery rites, that were heresy in their time, have been disguised in the extraordinarily elaborate stone carvings.

1905047924 260pp b/w + colour illustrations **£19.95 $29.95** cl